I0186455

Seven years ago I was here.

flipping through, over and under old breaths taken.

I felt one from an old poet love of mine.

I'm no longer who I was but words and breath will

always be.

Twenty – five.

A frown longer than a deserted highway in mid august

Dust at the corners as if it were stranded for years

Seamless and flawless and beautiful and tragic

Her ponytail danced while the wind

Forcibly tried to take her down

A swing set built strictly from pain

And bricks

And kicks to the head because she didn't smile enough

Or play with the boys the way they wanted her to play

She's in her twenties now.

Changes.

The crab-apples want to be red delicious

The maples want to be ivy

And I want to sit under a different sky

And listen to different sounds

As my body falls into sleep

The highways want to be wider

The bridges, higher

I want to swing lower on this block

Of wood made of lies and thoughts, lost

The branches want to be longer,

To be able to grab a hold of the wind

And shake it harder

The grass wants to be taller

I will hide inside and be shyly

Aware of all that is alive.

I believe.

Everyone wants something worth believing in.

I believe in my skin

Now

I believe in my breath

Whether shallow or heavy

I believe in my fingertips

Confident in the way they touch

Feel, see with their own little eyes

I believe in my love

Now

I believe in my gut

Whether right or doubting

I believe in circles traced

And obstacles

Tripping, kicking, tackling one thing

Or another

I will not ask, nor beg

To be believed in

I believe in contrast and satisfaction

In dead ends and everlasting highways of emotion

In sadness and pure happiness

In falling ashes and broken glass

I believe in something

Now

I believe in air

And ground and dirt and roots

I believe in clouds

I believe in things that are far away now

Intangible and impossible

No need to see or grasp or taste

I am constantly diving

Dancing beneath my poker face

Entangled and restless

I don't need someone to believe in

I don't need someone to believe in me

I believe in deserted stretches of shore

I believe in mountains and lust and poetry

In radio stations while traveling nowhere

In carnivals and costumes

In flowers and trees and collar bones and knees

I believe in ankles and spit

Everyone wants something worth believing in.

And you can share my wild fantasies

Of women bathed in freckles

I believe in scars and stories

In sincere excitement

In chapters and in empty pages

Faeries and mermaids

And I believe they speak

In an unknown language you have to choose

To understand

Comprehension

Revelations

Unending frustrations

I believe in forever

When it comes to certain things

Music

Holding hands when it's pouring rain

Staying in bed until the sun sets again

I believe in dreams

And reincarnation

Tickle fights and pillow fights

And fist fights

And make up sex

Anger and humiliation

Relaxation and hibernation

I believe in life

For the first time in mine.

Unaware

I don't know what cobblestone feels like

Under naked feet, arched and aching for texture

For warmth or to be cold

Internally cold, nothing a sweater could cure

To be radical; to scream so loud that rooftops shake

Pressing fingertips to fingertips unknown

I don't know the smell of tropical air

I've flown, but never took in the air around me

Consciously.

I'm unaware of the pain that is not mine

I'm unaware of the pain that is.

Buttons.

Push my buttons

I'm an elevator and you want to go down

Kiss me until I bleed, and rub me until I'm raw

To be worshiped like a statue in rome

To be challenged like I'm in the corner of a ring

Goosebumps sailing across my back like an ocean storm

A hundred years of temptation in minutes

Starving to be fed, let me shake until after it's over

Turn me inside out and taste what is my being

Show me what you know and what you strive for

Teach me what you love and what you'd die for

Trace the snake of my spine with possessed fingers

Trace the scar on my neck with your tongue

Emotions spiraling into delusion

Completely content without the confusion

Just turn me over and make me proud

Back and forth and up and down

Our bones are making music

Our breaths are writing poetry

And for that moment I'm willing to give all of me

Raspy and warm, sweaty and swollen

Freedom will drip down our chests

And my thighs will be bruised

And sore in that good way

Going 80 miles per hour down your highway

I just want to be felt at the core

That's really all I'm asking for.

Grace.

I haven't walked much since.

The trees passed by me, through me

Moved around me, gracefully

Like a Native American dance.

Through pictures

I realize how my cheeks shine

When being bathed in the outside light.

My crooked smile

In those moments

Seemed to fit just right.

Circus.

You string words together like cheap costume jewelry

Parade around in this make believe circus that no one is really watching

That no one would dare buy tickets for.

Underneath this façade you create

You are just another bleeding artist

The sky when there's nothing left to look at.

The ground when there's nothing left to trip on.

Revelation.

The sweet taste of dedication

Or desperation

Or temptation

Or pure revelation.

Everything spiraling

Into another

Tumbling down over

Mowed over flowers

Grass staining

The only good pair of jeans

 I have left.

Take a sip of forever

And spit out a little at a time

And underline every feeling

that dominates my mind.

Science.

The days.

Oh, the days...

When I could let my limbs flop

My words would fall onto my bed sheets

Like articles about the never ending science

Of the human mind

You are science.

I would study you

Hands on

If I had the chance to.

Eight years.

So this is what I get.

So this is what you give me.

Eight years

I've been raising a daughter

With strong bones and

Fierce eyes

And

This is what I get.

No explanation of your permanent vacation

No new theories that would prove my ideas false

No "how has she been?" or "does she look like me?"

This is what you give me.

"you have a new friend request".

Eight years and you befriend me on a social networking website?

Eight years worth of laughter and tears

Of punishments and awards for good behavior

Eight birthdays.

Eight winter solstices.

Eight years of nothing

And you come back with this?

This is what I get.

This is what you give me.

The tooth fairy is finished.

Santa Claus is almost over.

She's getting boobs and has a crush on a boy.

She sings and dances and gets straight A's in school.

She makes me cards for no reason other than she loves me.

She is empathetic and sarcastic.

She is hilarious and powerful.

She is wise and brave and beautiful and free.

She got all of that from me.

I know.

He knows

How breath means more to me

Than flowers

How words tickle me

That a sentence

Can make or break me

Silently

And he knows

How to stir my insides

With "good morning, beautiful"

And that his arm enveloping me

In the quiet night

Makes me feel safer

Than I have ever felt before

And he knows

That I silently promise

To be his forever

He knows how to love me

Like no one ever has

No one has ever

Tried

When I begin to fall

He knows

Which parts to catch

And which parts to let go.

The real kind.

The shape of our spines

Entangled in, what can only

Be described as

Raw, intense, beauty

Raw love.

The real kind of love

That bends to fit

And shares a breath

Hungry at the same time

For the same thing.

I want.

Just a warm place

Where the sky opens up

And words stream out

Collapsing

And twisting up limbs

As if a story is to be written

At once

A full glass

Of red wine on green grass

Dancing orange blossom dream like

Wonderings

Wandering inward to find

What tastes so sweet

Tangible or not.

9:22pm

Tornado winds

Rustling words through

A frayed mind, which

Hardens the need to

Breathe evenly.

Coffees' steam has

Long disappeared, cold

Draft coming in from

The right and it

Is quiet.

In here.

When I can't see behind your skin, I panic.

Because bread crumbs can only get me so far

And while I look at you and see the stars

I can only look so long

Before my vision goes blurry and the darkness starts

And while my fingertips long to touch your skin

And my skin longs for your fingertips

I can't seem to find the piece of string that
connects them

Did we lose it in the chaos of living?

I'm scared.

The butterflies never left

And when you graze my arm on accident

Goosebumps appear

'cuz those tiny bumps? They live in here.

I find myself apologizing for wanting to be your lover

And each time I say "I'm sorry", I die a little more inside

Trying to decide

Which side

To sleep on

Is turning my skin into leather and

We could blame the weather

But it's only been raining for two days

And the rain is supposed to wash away the hurt;

Replenish what lives underneath the dirt…

10:15pm

Eyes closed

Counting the mile markers

On the road to somewhere

We all want to be somewhere.

Where the water tastes like freedom

And the locals don't stare.

Fresh fruit is currency

Arms to wrap around you

Ears to listen to

You

Nothing is scary

Everything is

Beautiful.

Listen.

Listen

To me like you

Listen to

The wind as it spirals in every direction

At night when you can't keep yourself from rejection

No matter how

Hard you try.

Fingering ideas because they're only ideas

And my mind works better than I do.

But my mind is still worth listening to, through

Fucking frustration over endless illustrations

That have mapped themselves over my bones

I can feel more when I'm alone.

Shutting down like the interstate when a truck flips
on its back

There's nowhere to go so we just sit there.

And stare.

Things will start moving soon.

Nothing that we can do

But listen.

Live.

It's behind me.

The pulsing rhythm of the earth /

Silent echoes of my past.

It surrounds me.

The heavy drops of liquid sky /

Redundant whispers of my core.

Nedra.

Words are what we've got.

We will speak of you

Quote you

And tell stories

About you.

Music will be your breath.

The piano; your face

The keys; your fingers

The song; your laugh

The shore will be our photo album

Our children are your eyes

Our tears; your kisses

(they'll live on our cheeks eternally.)

We saw yellow butterflies

The morning after

Within arm's reach

They were

And you will

Forever be.

Babies.

Out of my womb

Came two

Beauteous and electrifyingly

Powerful

Babies.

She:

Courageous

Intelligent

Witty

Unafraid to be.

I can't wait to see more.

He:

Strong

Mellow

Still in diapers.

I can't wait to learn more.

Giving life to these children has given meaning to mine. I love you both more than rainbows.

www.ingramcontent.com/pod-product-compliance
Lightning Source LLC
Chambersburg PA
CBHW031219090426

42736CB00009B/993